Prayers for Faith Meetings

Rev. Dr. Claudia A. Ramisch

DEDICATION

To Mom

CONTENTS

ACKNOWLEDGMENTS

THANK YOU: Kevin Karl & Marilyn Duncan
For immediate assistance
THANK YOU: Unitarian Universalist Congregation of Owensboro
For calling forth my pastoral ministry

1 TIPS & SUGGESTIONS

Prayers for Faith Meetings is intended for use by faith groups that include either a meditation or prayer period in their meetings. It is my conviction that every faith group—even finance boards!—should begin meetings with a time of reflection and close with some blessing words because it is one of the clearest ways to demonstrate our difference from social and political clubs. It is also one of the easiest ways to remind ourselves that our business in faith is not just business.

Anyone can use and lead these prayers—from committee chairs to clergy, from volunteers to professionals. Very few props are called for (except a candle now and then) but you can and should add what's appropriate in your setting. Here are some things you should know about the formats:

- The term *prayer* is defined this way: Reverent attention to the mysteries of life. It is not presumed that all people who use these will address their prayer *to* someone. It is presumed that all users are thoughtful and reflective before the wonders and worries of our human life.

- These are mostly generic interfaith prayers: No special titles for Divinity or Meaning are used. Please add what is appropriate for your setting! If you have a group of only one or two faiths, make the prayers specific by using the titles preferred by those groups. If you have a group of many faiths, work with your group to determine what is best for them. Do not ignore that there are differences nor that the differences matter. In some cases, no titles will be the way to go. But some groups prefer to include all the important titles among them or to alternate titles over the course of several meetings.

- Please make sure your group understands that interfaith prayer and sharing is not a fluffy exercise. Different traditions use terms differently and we can easily say something that offends another's sensibility without malicious intent. Please ask members to be generous in asking for clarifications or naming their difficulties—as well as accepting of differences that may not be changeable.

- If your group consistently uses a scripture or music in its reflection, feel free to add that to the format. (Possible references are not included simply because there are too many possible Sacred Texts and hymnals from which to draw!) Recorded music is mentioned in a couple of the Longer Reflection services—but no specific suggestions are given. Choose what is suitable for your group.

- Now and then, people are inappropriate when they speak off the cuff. Usually this is rare, but if someone is regularly disrespectful of listeners or the process, it should be addressed before it taints the spirit of reflection for the group. Please be kind but direct when you speak with someone about this. However, a larger concern is when someone blurts out something bigger than your training or the group's capacity. If something surfaces in group sharing that troubles you, seek counsel or professional assistance. Do not let the individual or group languish.

- If you have someone who continually dominates a group or engages in crosstalk, choose a way to limit sharing. Of course, it is preferable if you can speak with the person of concern directly and ask for cooperation in letting others have the floor. If that's not possible or it's unsuccessful, some other options include:
  o Limit sharing time per person
  o Use a talking stick
  o Make a practice: No one can speak twice till all have had the chance to speak or pass on speaking
  o Write answers and allow the leader to read them

Format Cues for *Prayer for Sharing Hearts* and *Longer Reflections*:
Silence Obviously this means be quiet! But the key is to be quiet as long as your group can be still. Our world has too much noise and too many words for us to hear our hearts well. So offer participants time to be quiet together; it will deepen your group's work.

_____ This means the leader should provide appropriate information or give directions for others to fill in that blank.

Name or mention something here This means the entire group should be invited to participate. Usually this means they are invited to say something; take your time with these exercises.

Prayer & Sharing This means that some form of sharing or group participation will be included.

Pastoral Prayer This means that a leader will read the text and that there isn't any planned verbal sharing. The term is intended to convey the spirit of the prayer not the person to lead it; the leader does not need to be a pastor or a religious professional.

Benedictions & Prayers/ Readings & Poems
Texts that are formatted with two types of print (standard and italic) are prepared for responsive reading. The standard type is intended for One Voice or Leader and the *italics are intended for the Many Voices or the Assembly.* Some of the poems refer to God and are more personal than the group formats.

Special Note:
These prayers were written in a Unitarian Universalist context. There are references to covenant and chalice that may be foreign to other groups. These are significant symbols for us .

Covenant refers to the promises a local community makes amongst its members that actually form that community. It is the most important "document" of a group's founding and describes the relationship to which members aspire. In our Congregation, our founders actually made a retreat together to write a statement that we use as part of our worship every Sunday. When we pray it together, we are reminded of our Congregational identity. In the prayers in this book, consider *covenant* to mean the promises your group makes to each other.

Chalice refers to a candle in a cup or bowl resembling a chalice goblet. It is a reminder of several things, among them: Our longing to know the light of truth, our commitment to follow the light within us, our promises to gather together in our pursuit of meaning, and our desire to burn in service to our neighbors. To light a chalice, is to physically light the candle representing these things. If your group or tradition uses a different kind of candle or lamp, feel free to substitute it.

Most Importantly
ENJOY! Being together, even in solemn and trying times, is a privilege. Appreciate each other and be faithful to growing your spirits together.

2 PRAYERS FOR SHARING HEARTS

These prayers all have consistent elements:

1- Introduction
   If this is a special occasion it can be acknowledged here
   Or you can simply mention what the purpose of the meeting is

2- Silence
   Let this be as substantial as your group can tolerate

3- Sharing needs or worries and hopes or joys
   Sometimes this is done with separate times for needs and joys
   Sometimes this is done with creative activities
   Sometimes this is couched in the prayers and blessings

4- Prayers for the world and blessings for the group

5- Closing words to use at the end of the meeting

NEW YEAR'S TIME

We begin again, yet again.

And we pause to consider what that means.

What are we leaving behind? What are we facing?

What are we taking up?

    Silence

Tell participants you will pause at the end of each phrase so they may name anyone who fits that description. They may do this silently or aloud.

We celebrate the life and work of who died this past year.

We delight in the joy of neighbors celebrating _____

We bless all who are beginning new terms at school

    and taking up healthy habits for the New Year.

We uphold the work of local shelters, relief agencies, clinics

    and social services working to make our city

    healthier, safer, and a better home for all of us.

We support those in public service engaged

    in changing dangerous neighborhoods for the better.

We remember with hope those in war zones.

We encourage those beginning spiritual quests and holy journeys.

We hail those striving to be true to health, recovery, wellbeing,

    piety or humankindness.

We bring those who are absent into our gathering by fond memory.

Wherever darkness remains in our hearts,

    we shine a candle of desire for change on it.

May we disperse all that causes anxiety and drags us down.

We look to the stars for hope, for strength to dream, for new visions.

May we hearten our aspirations and affirm our best selves

    in this hallowed gathering and in all we do together.

Closing Words

It is good to recollect our spirits on the cusp of a new year!

May we be refreshed by this reflection together.

May we be re-oriented to our path and our work.

May we begin again with each other's love and support.

HIGH ASPIRATIONS
REV. DR. MARTIN LUTHER KING, JR. OBSERVANCE

We take time to share some of the needs of our own lives.
But in this sacred moment, we do not turn in only on ourselves.
Instead we open ourselves to the needs of our world
    and call to mind our highest aspirations.
    Silence

Prayer & Sharing

Here we are gathered around our dreams of a better place:
    Where things are more even than not;
    where oneness is palpable; where service is our creed...
We allow the dreams of Martin Luther King Jr. to challenge us
    to bring our dreams to life sooner rather than later.
We allow his ministry to wake us up to our neighbors
    who need jobs with real wages and benefits
    rather than think only of our own hopes, or fears, or comfort.
We allow his words to confront us when we would rather compromise
    with second-class care for the oppressed, the sick, the poor,
    the homeless, the unseen and unnamed neighbor.
We allow his legacy to dare us to work non-violently
    for all who are at risk of violence, abuse, and crime.
We gather together our joys and concerns and those of our neighbors.
    Name special needs in your city...
Like King, we acknowledge frailties and failures and uncertainties
    sometimes in the face of overwhelming need,
    sometimes as a product of weariness.
But we are also brave and today we allow his vision to wash over us.
May it strengthen our compassion. May it test our mettle for change.

Closing Words

May we always unite our needs to the pains and pleasures
    of all of our neighbors.
May we take up the vision of Martin Luther King Jr.
    and bring our highest aspirations to life.

VALENTINE'S DAY

Love, love, love. This holiday can seem so sappy!
Let us be still before the deep potential and enduring power
of committed and faithful love in all its forms.
Silence

Prayer & Sharing

We have enlarged our hearts in the quiet of meditation
now we open our concern to those who are not here today.
We send the energy of our gathered love to our family, friends, and
neighbors for Valentine's Day.
Name them here…
We pray for our children that they will learn loving ways
to be friends, to care for the earth, and to attend to their neighbors.
Name them here….
May our dearest ones be sustained by deep and abiding love.
We send the hope of healthy, loving relationships to
those without family and friends, those in abusive relationships,
those struggling with loneliness and despair.
We bless those trying to preserve love in war zones—
Whether they are combatants, refugees, or peacekeepers.
Name or remember them here…
May those in need of renewed love be blessed today.
We extend blessings to the LGBTQ community
working for full civil rights for their loving relationships.
We draw into our care those whose love
shapes lives of community service and justice-making.
We celebrate those whose passion for the arts
gives us many beautiful expressions for love.
May we learn to extend our love through their examples.

Closing Words

Let us continually enlarge our hearts with loving reflection.
Let us be faithful to our healthy loves and reform unhealthy habits.
Let us serve those in need with loving thoughts and actions.

WINTER –SPRING, LIFE -DEATH

It's cold. I hurt. I am distressed. I'm dying and the path is narrowing.
It's warm. I heal. I am delighted. I'm living and things are expanding.
The poet says life and death are "woven fine,"
> no finer than this edge of winter-spring.

Whether we feel like we're living or dying, let us open our hearts
> to the joys and sorrows, hopes and fears of our community.
> *Silence*

Pastoral prayer

The dance of winter-spring-life-death is all about us.
We draw into our care all who are teetering between life and death.
> We join them in the dance of sorrow and hope.

We are also of the wider faith community dancing this transitional time
> with traditional feasts: Passover, Hola Mohalla, Easter, Holi.

And we are of the wider human community struggling to learn
> the steps of the dance of life-death.

So many things seem insurmountable:
> The slow social change, attitudes of ignorance,
>> out-of-control addictions, a decade of war...
> Abusive parents and partners, overwhelming workloads,
>> broken service systems...

How are we to set forth revived and renewed when all this drags on us?
Start with what is practical and be true to the process.
Let us give our meeting time today to making choices for life through
> the practical tasks and long-term loyalty to revival and renewal.

Closing Words

Between the insurmountable and the easy is the natural—
> The interplay and ever repeating cycle of life, death, life, death,
>> and always life.

Let us gather up our pains and healings in one holy basket of life.
Let us carry this basket together so that the daily deaths
> and life-beating events cannot isolate us or defeat us.

Let us walk together choosing life even in death.

SPRING GREENING

There have been hints and hopes, intimations and intuitions in the air...
>   A crack, a drop, a whiff.

As we near the date of Spring, we see it already springing...

And Spring is particularly audacious, dazzling,
>   even chaotic when it bursts into our consciousness.

But we have the sense to take time to stop!

To not rush headlong into it but to contemplate and share
>   The delights and pleasures we bring with us fresh as Spring.

And we take time, too, to recall the fragility of life and its struggles.
>   Not all that buds will come to fruition; not all that rises will stand.

Thus, we have the sense to share our worries, fears, and doubts as well.

Let us open our hearts
>   to receive the joys and concerns of our community.
>   ***Silence***

Pastoral Prayer

Fresh and flush, even the air, rain, and last snows smell new.
>   They stir our noses and tickle our souls!

We draw in this new air to fill our spirits, to lift our worries,
>   and elevate our joys—spoken and unspoken.

We breathe this new life upon all those we love
>   and those who are absent.
>   *Name them here...*

Spring greening fills the early festivals of the season—
>   ...the Irish dancing and drinking around Patrick,
>   ...the Italians breaking bread and blessing families around Joseph,
>   ...the Pagans coloring eggs for Ostara
>   ...and the Baha'i sharing nuts of Naw Ruz—

Oh how wonderful is our faithful world
>   that can celebrate in so many ways and touch so many people!

Oh how grand our planet that nourishes us;
>   oh how grand our creativity that extends the gifts of earth—

We innovate our life in music and melody,
    arts and ales, dances and dreams...
We intensify it in thought and ritual and table fellowship...
Just a bud of hope and we improvise a thousand ways
    to slough off our winter weights.

But look closely at the buds—struggling against late frost,
    driving rain, and abusive wind—
Let us be reminded of the fragility of neighbors in need
    trying hard for a fuller life.
Let us be reminded of the struggle of our friends
    with addictions and depressions and chronic illnesses
    whose lives never seem to break into bloom.
Let us be people who "guard with tenderness those without words"—
    Those who desperately desire to grow to full leaf and fruit
    but whose resources are limited.
    Name concerns and worries here...

As we enjoy the newness in and around us,
    as we spend ourselves helping others to bloom and flower,
    we are spring greening.
Hildegard von Bingen called this *Veriditas*: Truth greening in life.
We are life ever turning. *Today* we are life finally taking hold of the light.

Closing Words
May we appreciate the possibilities of our own lives:
Yes, let us trim and prune, till and spruce, feed and water
    what we are charged to tend
Not that the world think we're pretty but that our life
    be marked by health and hardiness.
Together, may we live a life of truth greening a grey world.

EASTER

An ancient Christian writer said,
> "Nothing in the universe is exempt from resurrection."

We aren't always happy about that.

Perhaps it's good to remember resurrection comes after death.
> Real death.

We have burdens and woes we need to put down and leave.
> We have soul-aches we need to let go of...

Let us take time today to help the dying process
> for the things that are of death.

And then let us also be attentive to that which begins to live anew.
> We have joys and hopes, dreams and buds of dreams.

> We have enjoyed success and surprises this week.

Let us take time to celebrate and nurture the things that are of life.

Let us open our hearts to the dyings and risings
> of our gathered community.
> ***Silence***

Prayer & Sharing

We gather into our care those who are absent—
> Traveling for the holidays or Spring Break,
> working, caring for the sick and dying, resting.
> *Name them here...*

May they have all they need today!

As death looms about us—
> in war, threats and rumors of war around the world...
> In neighborhood violence and toxic relationships...
> in addictions and abuse...
> In debilitating pain and depression...
> in the chokehold of systemic injustice...
> *Name any hotspots in the world or problems here...*

We resist coercion and oppression and revenge.

No, no, we do not resist the reality of our transience
only works of wickedness.
We would choose only the deaths of darkness and evil and depravity.
We would bless the natural deaths, the hard choices with mortality,
and the end of life decisions.
Name those facing death or life-changing decisions...
Indeed, as death asserts its power,
we stand together in covenant and choose life.

Yes, yes, we choose a power stronger and truer than death.
We choose life and refuse to be isolated from health and wholeness.
We choose life and its habits of right relationship:
Discernment and honesty,
graciousness and kindness,
loyalty and steadfastness.
We choose life and walk paths of justice
to assure all people's basic needs are met.
We bless those who do the hard work for public health and life.
We bless those who join us in charity and justice.
Name them here...

May our gathering be lifegiving.
May we be attentive to the impact of our planning and decisions
on the cycle of life-death-life in our community.
May an Easter awareness of resurrection pervade our work.

Closing Words
For today, and for the children, and for all living things without voices,
and for the generations to come beyond counting or knowing...
In the company of caring and vigorous friends:
We bless death in its necessity. We choose life in its endurance.
Together we commit to live Easter:
to make it real in love and grace for all that is fragile,
to make it real in love and grace for all who are vulnerable.

THE LAMP

What are we to do with the grief and happiness
    oozing at the edges of our hearts?
Here's what I recommend: Capture the grief and compress it with hope
    till it bursts into flame to light a candle to dispel our darkness.
Scoop up the happiness in a glowing ball
    to light a candle multiplying the brightness of this gathering.
Make of your pains and your promises a lamp to a better life.
Let us join you in this endeavor.
    Silence

Prayer & Sharing

We draw near in heart all those who are absent—
    Light a candle here.

The light we have lit is precious but it cannot be contained.
There is a hurting world that needs it…
    Mention any tragedies or disasters in the news
    Mention any personal or local concerns

We cannot keep our light only to ourselves.
    As we share the light with these troubled neighbors, it will grow.
It will grow and bless
    even more than those we call to mind here today.

Nor can we shine this light only in the painful, worrisome corners of life.
We must light up the hopes trying to break out.
We must illuminate little enjoyments, and small victories,
    and the everyday pleasures of our lives that they may grow.
    Mention any good news here
    Mention any personal celebrations or successes

Let us light torches on the square and invite others to dance with us—
At history museums and 12-Step meetings and drum circles...
    and all places that sustain our spirits.
At festivals and spray parks and art exhibits ...
    and all places that teach us re-creative play.
At church and in our kitchens ...
    and all places that nurture us and shape our character.
Let us light those torches so that in sustenance, play, and nurturing
    we will ease the stress of our society.

Celebrating life we will also nourish our spirits for the work of justice.
May we never forget, that the lamp of truth within us
    joins with the light we offer others in all these settings.
Let us nurture it and share it now and in our meeting.

Closing Words

Our light is precious: the light in our gathering, the light in our hearts.
As we go forth, may we be conscious we are light-bearers.
May we be a lamp of truth and justice,
    of hope and renewal, of assurance and encouragement
    for all whom we meet and serve.
So be it.

MEMORIAL DAY

Come, gather your hearts into this place!
Make haste to set down your burdens,
    unpack your worries, and release your anxiety.
    You don't need to hold them alone.
Come swiftly to this circle of care with your gladness and enchantment.
    We need to hear your happiness.
Come gather your hearts! Come open your hearts—
    to give, to receive the joys and concerns of the week.
    Silence

Prayer & Sharing

We send the light of our company with all who are traveling
    or recreating for Memorial Day weekend.
As a nation, we use Memorial Day to remember war dead
associated with far-off places:
    The 6758* casualties of Afghanistan and Iraq;
    the 58,220 of Vietnam; the 36,516 of Korea;
    the 521,915 in the two World Wars.
And we remember the 625,000 dead here at home
    in the Civil War that originated Memorial Day.
We remember all those who gave their life in service of their country
    in other war zones.
    Name any relatives or friends killed in war...

We remember those in need without voices to name their worries
    in community or society—
    Name concerns here...
We have created a circle where all their cares are joined to ours.

We use the power of this place and circle
    to bless all who put their lives on the line for fellows in need.
We bless all who serve the common good.
We bless all who are advocates and allies for our oppressed neighbors.

We look to our heroes and prophets
    to teach us the work of harmonious relationships.
    Name heroes and prophets here...
    Insert religious feasts that fall in late May & early June...
Here, this place, is a safe place where we ask questions of meaning
    and ponder values and shape attitudes
    that we might give our children a harmonious world.

Here we welcome the unspoken hopes and germinating joys.
In this place we dare the dream of one people where peace is normal.
In this place we dare the dream of one land
    where we leave footprints only till the next wind.

Closing Words
May this circle we have fashioned
    be incarnated in the larger community.
May it be a sphere of good influence
    extending our good intentions into good practices
    for health and wellbeing for all the earth.
We join our efforts to all people of goodwill and responsibility
    that all people may have their burdens lifted and rights upheld...
    that society will no longer think of war as an option...
    that generations to come will no longer mourn war-dead children.

* This number is current as of 09/19/13. Data can be found at:
    http://icasualties.org/

SOMETIMES GRACE

Sometimes grace floods us with pleasure and bliss.

But sometimes grace has a surprisingly sharp edge to it.

We need it to be so to pare away the barrier guarding our dreams,

    To demand our care when we'd rather turn our heads away.

And sometimes grace is soft and pleading

    Pulling our fears to the surface to free them,

    Pulling our compassion out of a zippered pocket to help another.

We take this time to remember some of the ways grace

    has touched us this week.

To recall how our complacency has been unsettled

    by delight or challenge or worry.

    Silence

Prayer & Sharing

We have meditated on the joys and concerns of our week.

In this simple way, we have called forth grace—

    Grace already planted in our hearts and present in our gathering.

Let us be awake in grace!

Let us name our concerns
    so we might encourage each other when spirits flag.
    Name concerns...
Let us name our joys
    so we might celebrate each other in success.
    Name joys...

Awake in grace, may we engage our neighbors in need.
    We multiply our inner abundance by slathering grace
        on wounded souls and troubled minds...
    We ease the strife of our world by pouring grace
        on conflicted relationships and dangerous homes...

Awake in grace, we make of our community life a mission
    to share our vision of a just society.
We express our fullest gratitude for the grace we enjoy
    by joining the work of a just society
    that feeds and houses, educates and employs all its citizens.
We unite the work of this group to the gratitude of our hearts.
Awake in grace, we work together on this mission.

Closing Words
Awake in grace, we make of our lives:
...A quest into hope...
    We dare to imagine peace in _____
...An adventure on a trail of promise...
    We dare to follow our inner convictions and dreams to _____
Sharp, strong and fierce; pleading, gentle and patient:
    Grace has brought us together and bound us in mission.
May the grace we share and the work we do together
    continue to be a blessing to the world.

LOVE SONGS

Love songs permeate the early summer air!
A healthy and rich life is full of all sorts of loves songs.
Love songs are best Bel-Canto, in the right range
      with lovely phrasing and true pitch.
          Perhaps touching and poingnant—just not sappy.
But love songs sung in too low a range are dark and raw—
      like those dear to us who hurt us and grieve us.
And love songs sung falsetto don't ring true—
      like those near to us that reinforce self-doubt.
We bring our hearts together at this table.
We pour out the pain of songs sung badly–by us, to us—
      and we name the need for healing—
      to modulate and resolve the dissonant things in our lives.
We disclose the delight of songs sung beautifully—by us, to us—
      and we celebrate in concert.
We bring our songs together at this table.
      Silence

Pastoral prayer

We gather into our hearts and our circle the love songs
      of those who are absent and all of those unable to sing.
We remember, too, those whose songs are laments this week:
...Communities at risk in war, economic collapse, epidemic illness,
      gang intimidation, drug violence...
...Individuals suffering in those communities as refugees,
      war widows and widowers, orphans and survivors...
...All those waiting for a missing loved one...
We remember folks struggling to find their voices:
... Addicts working to get or stay sober, unemployed workers,
      friends with abusive parents or partners....
We hum gentle mantras of healing to surround these communities
      and individuals with love and change.
Hum a verse of a song of healing here (e.g. There Is a Balm in Gilead)

We gather in our friends singing festival songs this week _____
Sing a verse of a seasonal song

We celebrate and encourage those who sing lullabies
and love songs to our children—
How blessed we are to know such people who prepare us
to hear love songs later in our life!
Hum a verse of a children's song here (e.g. Abide with Me)

And when we shout and stomp our feet,
a love song sounds like a triumphant hymn—
We shout and stomp for _____
Name personal celebrations and successes
Sing a verse of an appropriate party song (e.g. birthday) or
a favorite dance song

The air is full of love songs!
Let's ignore the sappy one and overcome the false ones
with our heartfelt melodies.
Let them set the tone for our work together.

Closing Words
Let's keep singing in the world!
Let's sing songs that buzz with life, that soothe the wounded,
that intone healthy changes deep within us and around us,
that renew and fill our spirits.
Let's compose new texts and tunes that offer our communities
evocative expressions for their deepest needs, truest loves,
and sacred hopes.
Let's keep singing as we go forth!

DEFY DESPAIR & DANCE IN THE SUMMER

Gathering our spirits to this time and place…

> *On the occasion of _____*

In sacred trust, we will offer to each other,

> the good news and bad news of the week.

We will offer the worries burdening us and the visions bursting from us.

In sacred trust, we will receive each other's hurts and hopes;

> we will receive each other's hearts and bless them.

We will include in care those outside our gathering.

Let us take time to listen inwardly and prepare our hearts.

Silence

Prayer & Sharing

We take time to share our burdens .

> *Invite participants to share their worries and concerns.*

We welcome the cares of our hearts that remain unspoken.

We also remember those who don't have safe places

> to share their hearts or whose security has been disrupted:

Citizens displaced from homelands as refugees…

Neighbors displaced from homes ravaged by natural disasters…

Friends displaced from family by abuse or addiction

> or mental illness or incarceration…

It is daunting to live in such a world

> where there's enough pain to go around!

We defy despair!

We extend the light and love of our gathering and our hearts

> to all these neighbors.

But we don't just live by defiance,

> we live by delight and the expectation of something new.
>
> *Invite participants to share their hopes and joys.*

We welcome the happiness of our hearts that remains unspoken.

We celebrate children at summer play
and community gardens feeding shelter residents.
We rejoice in events at the parks and block parties in the streets.
We play ball and build sandcastles and sit lazily on our porches.

We defy despair; we dance in delight.
We sing our faith with the exuberance of katydids!
We gather in those who are absent
and those who have requested our prayer or support.
We bring them here in thought; we surround them with light and love.
We allow the peace of this moment to douse our spirits like a sprinkler
and now we begin our work together.

Closing Words

What a blessing is our work together!
Let us go forth in peace to share the blessings of our time together.
Let us continue to defy despair, dance in delight, and sing our faith!
May this sacred trust we've shared help us to live well in the world.
Amen.

SUMMER BLESSINGS

From brilliant light and scorching heat to changeable wind and weather,
  it is summer and we like to imagine we are different for it.
But we are still packed with worries and wonderings.
We gather again with full hearts. Let us listen inwardly.
Silence

Prayer & Sharing

Let us share our concerns and joys with each other.
  Let us receive each other's hearts with care.
We bring to heart all those who are absent today.
We bring to mind all those unspoken needs of our lives.
What are we to make of the juxtapositions of these summer days?
So many summer observances like _____

 UN Day in Support of Torture Victims, Independence Day,
 International Day for Indigenous People, etc...
challenge us to ask deep questions in a season
that used to be associated with ease and vacations:

...What are we required to do
  to uphold each other and respect each other's rights?

...What does it mean to live safely with each other
  and be accountable for our freedom?

...What must we change within ourselves and society
  to assure the most vulnerable have all they need?

Somehow struggles are magnified by the heat.
    And needs are exacerbated by extreme weather.
Hot humid weather makes harsh news all the hotter, too.
Like the spray of a fire hydrant cooling a neighborhood:
...We claim the intensity of the season for our work for justice.

...We harness the extremes as passion for our charity
    and outreach to our neighbors.

...We transform the harsh and changeable images of the news
    by our inner meditation.

Like an old-fashioned day under a tree on the bank of a pond:
...We breathe gentle rest on all whose rights are at risk
    and whose lives are in danger.

...We send the light of refreshment and hope to our neighbors in peril.

...We bless children playing on their school break,
    students taking advantage of different kinds of school,
    and youth taking up summer jobs and internships
        to sustain and enlighten them.

We claim the light of refreshment and insight for ourselves, too.
    Mention any special celebrations or concerns here
Together, we transform summer angst to summer blessings
    that our work together may be fruitful!

Closing Words
May the summer blessings we have fashioned here
    continue to bear fruit in our hearts and homes.
May our work together be choice fruit in the summer's harvest.

POSSIBILITIES

Some days seem laden with potential; some seem drained of it.
What do you bring today?
Delight from your week and hope for the possibilities of this day?
Weariness from your week and sadness to set down?
> ***Silence***

Come into this circle of care and share your heart.
Come into this circle of care and hear your neighbor.

Prayer & Sharing

We draw into this circle of care all who are absent today
> and all we'll leave unspoken.

We bless our religious neighbors keeping feasts this week _____
Clearly, the blessings and promising possibilities of this day
> are not meant for us alone.

Let us imagine our circle of care extending
> to all the weariness and sadness far and near:

Discord in _____, violence in _____, and war in _____...
Losses and anniversaries of loss _____...
Friends struggling with addiction, chronic pain, unemployment,
> loneliness and _____.

There is grace enough to go around for all such weariness and sadness.
Let us share it first in our thoughts and in the strength of our gathering.

Let us also revel in the benefits our circle receives
> from the good works all around us:
> *Mention community projects and successes here*

Then, too, let us not neglect to care for the earth
> or marvel at her abundance and beauty.
> *Name some favorite beautiful spots in your area*

So many people working for good! So much beauty around us!
So much generosity and hospitality, encouragement and support!

The possibilities—
    for reviving the spirits of those who are flagging,
    for renewing families in pain,
    for restoring communities in strife,
    for forming just societies—
the possibilities are waiting
    for us to accept the grace offered to us in our gifts and skills
    and to gain the strength of our good will and committed effort.
Let us soak up the hope and help tendered to us;
    let us proffer our good will and effort to others.

Closing Words

May we greet the possibilities of our week with optimism
    …for we have gifts and skills to work with those possibilities
    …for we have hopes and dreams to match our skills
    …for we have each other
And somehow this combination is the beginning of a better world!

A BIGGER WORLD

We enter the door with our own burdens and responsibilities,
    pleasures and possibilities.
We take time now to share these—risking what is most troubling to us,
    accepting what is troubling another.
    Silence

In the speaking and in the listening, we rediscover
    that our individual orbits are smaller than we thought.
In this time let us enlarge our hearts
    in the give and take of each other's joys and concerns.

Prayer & Sharing

We open our care to all who are absent.
We draw into our meditation the bigger world:
    The troublesome stories in the news _____
    The anguish of our own lives _____
The constants: Unemployment, ignored addiction, domestic violence.
    Depression and grief and anxiety.
We do not take on the distress of others to weigh us down,
    but to offer a holy moment
    to breathe transformative power on them.
We surround these distresses
    with the light of inspiration and the energy of change.
We hold them only long enough to bless them
    and to bless the bigger world scarred by them.
We leave space in silence for all that is unspoken...

We extend our care to our religious neighbors keeping _____
    Mention any special feasts or observances or special events

We draw into our meditation the bigger world:
    The celebrations in our families and community _____
    The exciting plans and projects in our city _____
    The work that draws us to this meeting _____

Other good news: Scientific discoveries, medical progress,
    social changes, advances in civil rights,
    renewal and personal growth …
We do not take on the delights of others to hoard them,
    but to offer a holy moment
    to breathe in the transformative power within them.
We hold them within our sphere of influence
    just long enough to taste their blessing.
Then with gratitude we send them on as healing for the bigger world.

When we open our hearts to let in
    the joys and concerns of our community and of the bigger world…
When we let these things pass through our more compact quarters…
    We resist our isolation and widen our own views.
When we shun common resentments and deepen our grace…
    We also shape a healthier bigger world. So be it.

Closing Words
Let us leave this sacred space bigger in heart, bigger in concern
    and ready to work for the good of the bigger world.

SHINE ON

The enduring traditions love light!

They teach us to follow those who are light, to seek enlightenment,
>to shed the light of truth on our wounded world.

But they do not ignore the power of darkness.
>Sometimes darkness must be exposed, undone, and overcome.

>Sometimes darkness must be embraced as a womb.

Let us open our hearts to the light and darkness
>we carry with us today.

>*Silence*

Pastoral Prayer

We nurture the darkness of new life and rest with just enough light
>to encourage maturing.

Faced with dangerous darkness that seems too deep to penetrate,
>The tangles of tragedy, the pervasiveness of greed and violence,

>The anxieties of great need, the drama of broken lives....

We dare to pierce it together—*(Light candle here)*
>with the light of a small candle grown into a circle of care.

Light grows in this time we take just to be with each other
>and grows again in our work for a healthy and just world.

Certainly light will spark and startle us this week—
>in a belly-laugh with a friend or a good doctor's report,

>In a public meeting or a stout cup of coffee and quiet,

>in a dogwood in full breathtaking blossom, In the dance of life.

Oh how pleased we will be to see it in those brief, illuminating bursts!

Oh how we will want it to gather brilliance and shine on!

Shine on it will—as we savor and treasure it;
>as we commit to what matters personally and communally.

Closing Words

As we persevere in our work for a healthy and just world,
>light will shine on. LIGHT WILL SHINE ON!

Indeed, light will erupt in the committed service we offer our neighbors
>and our affirmation of the generous lives of others.

HIROSHIMA DAY & CIRCLES OF LOVE & PEACE

One hundred years ago, Edwin Markham famously wrote about
  someone else drawing a circle of exclusion and
  his choice to use Love to draw a circle of inclusion.
The Japanese choose to draw a circle of peace around Hiroshima Day.
We take time in our meeting
  to draw circles of love and peace around our joys and concerns.
  Silence

Prayer & Sharing

The pain and anguish out there is staggering.
I hardly have energy to work at healing what I can touch…
  What am I to do with that scale of violence?
What am I to do with the messiness of our own country and city?
Perhaps the very futility of my own effort is the key.
Together, let us stretch our concern
  beyond our immediate reach and restraints
And draw the world's aches into a circle of blessing in this gathering.
We enlarge the circle of love to include _____
  Mention any special events or concerns or religious feasts
We encircle with love all who are absent today.
  We encircle all that remains unspoken in our hearts.
We encircle with peace all the world's danger zones.
Let us unite our best intentions and our highest purposes so that
  together we have strength and goodwill
To bless warriors and refugees, perpetrators and victims,
  sinners and saints with grace—that unearned love
  that transforms darkness and awakens us all to a better way.
Let us draw circles of love and peace around our world.

Closing Words

May the grace we shared here
  inform the work of our hands in the wider circle.
May we always choose to draw circles of love and peace
  to heal the world in which we live.

WHAT CAN COME OF THIS?

What a wild and wondrous world in which we live!

We are pinched by worries and crushed by concerns

> even as we are uplifted by our dreams
>
> and inspired by the kindness of others.

Let us pause in this time and space to share what pinches or crushes us

> as well as what uplifts and inspires us.

Let us pause to hear what we bring in our hearts today.

> *Silence*

Pastoral prayer

We bless and enfold with care all who are absent today

> and all that remains unspoken in our hearts.

What can come of the violence in the world?

What can come of the wounding of earth in this age of climate change?

What can come of the fluidity of economics and social policy that leave

> the poorest at great risk and squeeze the middle class?

For that which is beyond our reach, let us give this moment to mercy.

Let us devote the reverent attention of our gathering

> to the gaping wounds around us that we
>
> may thwart the negativity that seeps into all we see and feel.

What can come of the beauty that surrounds us?

What can come of the delight of concerts in the subway?

What can come of children happily at play and busily at study?

What can come of lovers walking in the park after dark?

For that which is within our reach, let us give this moment to grace.

Let us draw on the power of our gathering

> to fill our spirits with hope and love.

Closing Words

What can come of our world?

What can we imagine for it? What are we committed to doing?

Now let us make common cause with people of goodwill

> and go forth shaping a better world.

LIFE IS A RIDDLE AND A MYSTERY

Part of what makes it possible for us to function in the world
    is our ability to claim our past memories
    and shed light on the riddles of meaning,
To name our hopes burning for the future
    and to find healing in our present.
We enter into the mystery of each others' lives
    by listening to each others' joys and concerns.
    Silence

Pastoral prayer

We are grateful for this time to gather and work together.
We extend the light of our blessed time to sad memories
and to the troubles that are riddles in the lives of those we love:
    Mental illness and addictions and loneliness...
    Undiagnosed illnesses and abusive relationships... And more.
So many forces in this world push us
    to betray our own power and responsibility.
As people of faith, we accept our power and responsibility.
We stand together and extend the light of blessing.
    Let us name those who need this light: _____
We also revel in the successes and festivities around us.
We bask in the light of _____ *(Name local celebrations)*
Before the riddle of pain and struggle,
Before the mystery of all that is on that human scale
    from irritating to overwhelming,
We stand together in power and extend the light of blessing.
May our work together be a source of light and hope!

Closing Words

May our personal dreams glow within us and our community efforts
    draw together the divine sparks we carry to shine great lights
    on the mysteries and riddles of life .
May our lives always shine a light on the good that is possible
    and the justice that is holy.

TO MAKE IT CLEAR

Life is hard. Life is grand.

Either way, it's complicated and messy, beautiful and challenging.

When we gather in covenant

we use this time to make it clear to each other in what ways

our lives are complicated and messy, beautiful and challenging.

We pause to reflect on our week just past and the week to come.

Then we name the hard things that worry or disturb our spirits.

And we name the grand things that uplift and delight us.

Together, we embrace the whole of life.

Then we set out to make clear to others,

How the world can be different—better!

Let us gather our thoughts.

Silence

Prayer & Sharing

Let us be open to the joys and concerns of each other's hearts.

We include in our remembrance those who are absent.

We gather into our circle the joys and concerns we bring with us

and bless them.

Name joys and concerns here...

We turn our thoughts to our mission together.

May our experiences confront us with constructive questions

that dare us to improve the world for everyone.

May our companions assist us in discernment

that tests our values and hammers them into useful tools.

By our spiritual work and our intellectual struggle

may we rooted in clarity of conscience and purpose.

Then let us turn our attention to the process of social justice

That our neighbors in danger zones may be preserved in life...

That our neighbors crushed by oppression be lifted up...

That our neighbors yearning for freedom of body or mind

or spirit be released...

We seek strength to live our callings fully.
>We seek clarity in our thoughts and direction
>and promise each other support on the way.

May we put the power of our convictions to work for others.

May we share power in community decision-making
>and care for the vulnerable.

May our lives individually and together make it clear that we are people
>true to our covenant and passionate in our mission
>who build healthy relationships and advocate a just society.

Closing Words

We leave here and return to the
>complicated and messy, beautiful and challenging world.

We leave here with more clarity about
>who we are and what we do in this world.

We leave here embracing the whole of life,
>prepared to make clear to others:
>the world can be better and we can make it so... together!

COME HOME

Home is a powerful image that evokes worst and best memories,
    highly anticipated and dreaded encounters.
It casts long shadows across generations and histories.
For the moment set all that aside and just come home to your self.
It has been a full and twisted week around us.
In this safe space, come home to your self.
    Silence

Prayer & Sharing

Come home to the delights and pleasures you've experienced this week.
Name them. Share them. Hear the same from others.
    Name the delights here...
Come home to the distresses and pains that have troubled you.
Name them. Share them. Hear the same from others.
    Name the distresses here...
We remember in our gathering all who are absent:
    May they have time to be at home in quiet in themselves.
Together let us go deeper still and rest in our true and whole selves.
We send healing light and holy energy on all that has been spoken
        and all still held in silence.
    Silence

Sometimes it is hard to muster the energy to get here,
        but when we gather and then take the time to center ourselves
        at home in a common core of grace,
We reach deep and listen with compassion
        to the cries and laughs of the earth and each other.
We share an amazing earth and the potential for a satisfying life,
        But it is so hard to see when the news is crazy:
        ...The tragedies of wounds and wars...
        ...The disappointments of failures and infidelities...
        ...The substandard survival of neighbors and nations...
        ...The throbbing of the earth in agony...
all these bend our hearts in anguish.

We need to be together to keep our balance,
  to cleanse our spirits, to regain our hope.
Blessedly, we teach each other that we are about more
  than the distortion of goodness and beauty.
When we are together, we are grateful for :
    ...Those that serve, sustain, and inspire our best selves...
    ...Those that protect people and prosecute danger...
    ...Those that sit in healing presence and wait in vigil with us
      to mend the distortions...
More so, when we are together, the circle of our inner home is enlarged
  and our souls are magnified by the promises we make
  and keep with each other.
When we are together, indeed we are reminded
  of the nurturing gifts of our natural home, Mother Earth,
  and the reflection of her virtues in our lives.
When we are together, we mirror the light within and without
  in our thoughtfulness, our openness, and our work together.
When we are together, we create a comfortable space
  for each other and for the ideas that inspire us.
We exult in the loveliness about us
  and we deepen our capacity for considerate care for it.
Oh the loveliness of this common core of grace;
  grace that is our home as we begin our work together!

Closing Words

We go forth in mission to serve those without homes—
  without somewhere to live, without a community,
  without a spiritual dwelling.
We go forth strengthened because we have soaked in the grace
  of this common home we have built from our promises.

AUGUST ISSUES

In our primetime together, we deliberately set aside time
> to listen to our hearts. This is that moment.

Let us enter into silence to examine our hearts .
> *Silence*

Prayer & Sharing

What do you need to offer us from your heart?
> *Name any worries or celebrations...*

Let us surround these and all unspoken thoughts with light and love.
Now let us turn our attention to the world outside us:
On 10 Aug 1846, President Polk signed the act
> establishing the Smithsonian Institution.

We celebrate the vision of the Italian scientist, Smithson,
> who bequeathed his estate to the US for this purpose...
> and we celebrate the scholars who have brought that vision to life.

On 11 Aug 1965, the Watts Riot broke out and continued for five days.
We remember with concern all the areas
> that remain economically and socially isolated—
> that are hotbeds of oppression in our nation.

From the Smithsonian's dedication to learning
> to the history of race and economic riots,
> we are a country full of diversity, blessings, and woes.

We are situated in a world chock full of diversity, blessings, and woes.
As we have named the interests of our own hearts,
> we are mindful our neighbors all swim in matters of consequence.

Let us join the groanings and songs of all people to our own.
Then let us enfold them with light and love
> and commit ourselves to healing the world.

Closing Words

History can hold the brilliant and innovative right beside
> the troubling and destructive. Sometimes our spirits can, too.

We go forth reminded of our ability to choose healing
> and the power of our work together for the sake of healing.

DO YOU HEAR?

Do you hear your heart? Are you attuned to its quiet anxiety and worry?
This week did you notice its little breaths of hope and excitement?
Or did you only pay attention when it screamed at you?
Stop for a moment. Listen to your heart. *Silence*
Stop again. Make your heart ready to listen to your neighbor. *Silence*
Now, with open and compassionate hearts,
>   let us receive the joys and concerns of our community.

Prayer & Sharing

There are little things that bother us that we don't name
>   because they seem so little.

But there are other things we don't name lest we give them credence.
We allow our unnamed troubles to come into this circle of care
>   and we tender our blessing to them.
>   *Name concerns here...*

We also offer this care to unnamed neighbors in distress and danger.
How good are our hearts to trouble us with trouble
>   and to direct us to compassion and to change.

Let us join the work of our hands to the care in our hearts.
Then let the gladness of our hearts inspire us to dance
>   with the little joys and the grand successes.
>   *Name delights here...*

Compassion prompts us to work, gladness to dance...
How good it is that we take time to listen to our hearts!
>   How good it is that we listen together!

Closing Words

It would be grand if our reflection and compassion were sufficient
>   to heal all the world's wounds...

But we know we need to put our hands to work for that to happen.
We have worked together here;
>   let us go forth committed to more work
>   for the causes that our hearts bring to our attention!

LET US BE STILL AND AT PEACE

We cannot go it alone and be healthy in this world;
     neither can we run at warp speed and be healthy.
Let us be still together, calling to mind the things that worry us
     that we need to set free.
Let us be still together, calling to mind the joys we need to share.
     Silence

Prayer & Sharing

Let us be still together with the needs of the world.
Let us surround these concerns with healing silence
     and set them free in peace:
     Silence

For discernment over policy regarding all places touched by violence...
For those still healing from 9/11, Benghazi,
     and for all people touched by terrorism...
For those overwhelmed by life's demands, by depression,
     or by loneliness...
For those who are exhausted or infirmed...
     Name any local concerns here...

Let us surround these lives of courage and commitment
with silent affirmation and set them free in delight:
     Silence

For the scientists in the Shelios Expedition observing the Northern Lights
     in Greenland—and for all scientists studying life's mysteries
     and opening paths of knowledge for us...
For the Tibetan Buddhist monks protecting endangered wildlife— and for
     all people acting on their deepest convictions for the good of all...
For local farmers and all who work to feed our citizens—and for
     all who love and tend the earth...
For friendship, companionship, and fidelity in relationships and for
     all who love and sustain us...

In the common and unusual, in the diversity of efforts,
in survival and healing, in birth and discovery
is the struggle to steadily apply concord to conflict.
As we work together, may the stillness we have gathered
keep us mindful of the big needs and our role in meeting them.
May we multiply the energy of peace within our own lives.
May our stillness be as a perch to peace cranes circling our homes.
And together may we encourage seeds of peace to grow in new grounds.

Closing Words

Who will slow down and be still?
Who will wait in the quiet and build a broader awareness of peace?
We will. As we have done here, we will do in our daily lives.
We will not be dissuaded from being who we are as peacemakers.

CHALICE LIGHT

We shine the light of our chalice on our anxieties and hopes.

We also gather in our unspoken worries and successes.

Let us be focused on this light that joins us together.

Let us be one in spirit as we enter into silence.

> *Silence*

Prayer & Sharing

We celebrate this lamp that represents our faith.

> We share the good things our faith has prompted this week: _____

We bless unnamed gifts with light to grow.

We nurture the flicker of new and unknown holy gifts.

We burn out what weighs us down.

In this light we see the needs of community and world together:

> We surround the grieving and sick with healing energy ...
>
> We bless our members who are absent and traveling...
>
> We hold in loving attention family and friends active in addictions...
>
> We bathe in the glow of peace the people in war zones...
>
> We turn the light of civility on our public discourse...
>
> We illuminate the need for deeper racial dialogue...

May we shine hope on our neighbors in need of the basics of life...

> in places of danger and distress...
>
> in moments of despair and desperation...

May this brightness reveal a way for our hands to be useful

> In changing these dark circumstances.

May the radiance of compassion grow in our hearts

> as our commitments to service in our neighborhood, our community,
>
> our region, our world grow in our daily lives.

Closing Words

Invested in bearing the light of our chalice to the world and

> encouraged by the work we have done together

We rise enlightened in compassion and a desire to serve.

We rise refreshed for outreach as we live our covenant.

BE IT AFFIRMED

We have chosen to be here.

We are committed to each other and a better world.

Let us breathe peace together.

> *Silence*

Now let us breathe peace on these intentions.

Tell participants you will pause at the end of each phrase so they may name anyone who fits that description. They may do this silently or aloud.

We are thankful for those who serve our community.

We challenge ourselves and our city to care
> for those in need of life's most basic goods.

We comfort those who mourn recent losses
> and all those with enduring grief.

We extend hope and light to places dark with danger and discord,
> war, abuse and violence.

We cast out the worries and discouragements of our spirits.

We nurture with grace the small projects and big dreams we hold.

We celebrate all whose birthdays and anniversaries are this week.

We include in our love those who are absent for work or weariness,
> health or family, travel or trouble.

We surrender the unspoken concerns of our hearts
> to the silent care of this community.

Be it affirmed: We will change this world with meditation,
> discernment and dialogue, outreach and service.

Closing Words

We have finished the work of our meeting.

We are prepared to leave here,
> but we remain committed to each other and a better world.

Be it affirmed: We will be peace in our world.

Rev. Dr. Claudia A. Ramisch

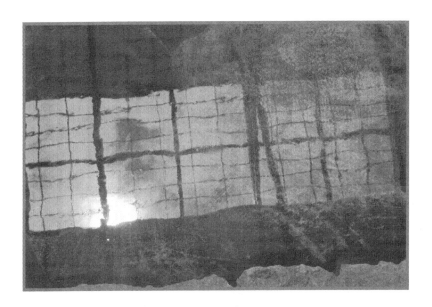

3 LONGER REFLECTIONS

These are services designed for use in 30 - 60 minute timeframes. In some cases added input on the topic is required to make them most effective.

Although they are not a small-group or covenant group curriculum, these services presume that your group either has enough comfort to share things that matter deeply to them—or that they want to become that kind of group. The basic ground rules at the beginning of "Tell Me a Story" should be operational for each service.

TELL ME A STORY

This service is built around time for storytelling. Make sure the group knows the ground rules before you begin:

- *Keep sharing brief.*
- *Don't force anyone to share.*
- *Focus on feelings more than details.*
- *Confidentiality is essential and can only be broken if someone reports abuse or threatens someone.*
- *Storytelling in this setting is a "non-feedback exercise;" listen, don't comment or offer advice.*

Opening Words

Tell me a story, tell us a tale—of how things are with you.

Set aside all that weakens you; share what braces you.

Tell us your mind and heart. Set your spirit free in the telling.

And then, let us bind our spirits one to the other

that we may all be stronger and truer to our covenant.

If your group has a behavioral covenant or foundational prayer,

recite it here.

Prayer & Sharing

We draw into our care those who are absent

that they may share our strength.

Let us also draw into our care all that remains unspoken within us.

The stories this week have been both heart-wrenching and heartening—

Violence, peacemaking. Loneliness, friendship.

Addiction, recovery. Unemployment, new jobs and careers.

It seems the world out there and the lives we lead

are painfully and incredibly similar.

Let us tend the stories we share with neighbors near and far,

with each other.

Let us take a moment to reflect on a story we need to share here.

Let it be a current story and one that can be told briefly.

When you tell your story, begin with this phrase:

The most important thing that happened this week...

If you repeat this service, change the opening line to suit your goal.

First let us prepare our hearts. *(Silence)*

If you repeat this service, you might play instrumental music here.

Now let us tell our stories forthrightly but without bitterness.

Let us tell them with sensitivity and simplicity

that all who desire to, may have time and space to share.

Let us listen with compassion

and remember to hold each other with tenderness.

Let us be open to insight wherever its found

and freely share the goodness that our lives reveal.

Allow time for personal stories

Thank participants for trusting each other

Benediction

Let us enfold these stories with grace and take from them wisdom.

Let us heal the broken spots in our stories and uplift their dark times.

Let us pray through them; let us surround them with light and love.

Let us be glad in the victories and successes of our stories.

Let us pray through them; let us take pleasure and love from them.

May our gathering be a sanctuary for our stories

and may we be a blessing to each other.

A BEAUTIFUL POEM

What has the world poured out on your life this week?
What joy is overflowing, what pain is spilling out?
How are the beloved ones around you?
> For what need should they be remembered?
> For what delights should they be celebrated?

Come, be still; then tell us what rises in your heart today.
> **Silence**

Prayer & Sharing

We gather close to us in spirit, those who are away in body...
> especially members of our community and family.

We call to mind the worries of the world
> and breathe a spirit of peace on them:
> Wildfires, earthquakes, flood and tornadoes ravage the earth...
> War, intimations of war, riots, espionage and crime destroy lives...
> Addiction without recovery, family violence and abuse...
> Debilitating depression and loneliness...

We breathe a spirit of peace upon the issues we bring with us: _____

Even with the weight of the world and the burdens of our lives,
> we know this is not the whole story.

We are amazing and resilient people with wells of inner courage.
We are faithful people in sticky and beautiful relationships:
> Families, friendships, communities...

We are realistic dreamers!
> Imagining new ways to beat back the troubles and survive.

We live on such paradoxical ground
> that sometimes only poetry can sketch our experience.

Even as we are mindful of our practical responsibilities to each other—
> our commitments to challenge and affirm each other
> and work together in this meeting—

Let's take up the artistic work of poets.
Let's sketch a beautiful picture of each other and our gathering
    with favored and potent words.
Yes, that's it! Let's share the words that describe and affirm us.

Have participants answer <u>some</u> of these questions
        What words inspire you in your difficulties? _____
        What words honor your struggles? _____
        What words celebrate you? _____
        What words describe your remarkable self? _____
        What words claim your aspirations? _____
        What words express your values? _____
        What words portray your spirit? _____
        What words comfort you? _____
Include time to discuss how you use these words
    and perhaps make a group tone poem.

Beloved, knowing these things about each other,
Having trusted each other with the language of our hearts,
May our work together always be a way we write beautiful poetry
    about our paradoxical and astonishing lives in the world.
May this poetry uphold us as we offer our lives in service. May it be so.

Reading: Choose a psalm or poem that is a favorite of your group
    and read it aloud here.

Closing Words
May we leave our meeting with new ideas and understandings
    woven into community poetry.
May our work continue in our minds and musings.
May the service that grows from this time together
    be a sacred poem reflecting the beauty of our paradoxical lives
    and our commitment to a better world.
May we help others to sketch their lives with honest and lovely words.
May it be so; may it ever be so.

HARD HISTORY

This service is intended for gatherings on anniversaries of significant historical events or as unusual things happen- locally or in the news. If the event is very close to home, consider inviting a bereavement counselor to facilitate or attend the session.

Be prepared to provide factual information about the event/ anniversary you plan to discuss. If your church or denomination has issued any statements about it, provide the material to participants. If the event is very recent, be sure to have the room arranged with drinking water, tissues, and a way for folks to walk around without disturbing the conversation. Prepare a Resource Sheet for participants to use after this session. Include more information about the event, resources for prayer, meditation and/or journaling, connections for support groups or therapists (if the wounds are particularly fresh or deep) and plans for any follow-up at church.

Our society gives so little time to quiet reflection
    on the history we have made and shared.
But together we have the chance to carve that time out of the week.
How wonderful it is for us to be together!
    To be together to share our hearts and give history our attention.

Let us set down and leave behind what we worries us. *(Silence)*

We bring to our attention all those who are absent. *(Silence)*

Let us call to mind what we treasure. *(Silence)*

Now let us take time to reflect on the historical events
    that are on our minds and hearts today.

Prayer & Sharing
How amazing is our human life: Rich and deep and full!
We grieve and wonder, worry and rejoice all at the same time—
    sometimes in the same thought.

Our responses to _____ are certainly varied.
We know how hard and cold the world can feel...
    how callous people can seem... how overwhelming news can be...
Yet we also have an incredible capacity
    to make sense of complex situations and
    to tend neighbors in danger or despair or need.
We are dedicating time to sorting out how we feel about _____,
    how we think about _____
    and what our faith has to say about _____
    --even if we aren't ready to work with that just yet.
Let us contemplate our needs and heed them.

1) Ask if anyone has any questions about the facts of the situation and provide whatever is available. Cite your sources. Don't be afraid to say, "It's too soon to know," or to stop speculation in its tracks. Ask participants to confine themselves to facts when they discuss the event with others. Remind them that speculation is really just a fancy form of gossip and can trigger unnecessary stress in a community.

2) Begin processing by sorting out emotional reactions to the event.
    If this is a first-time debriefing, expect this to be very raw . If this is
    an anniversary, consider including a question about how emotions
    have changed over time. Remind participants that they are to own
    their own reactions and not respond to or argue with someone
    else's response. Remember some people may have heightened
    reactions because of a connection to something else in their lives.

3) Continue by asking what questions or issues the event raises for *you*.
    Explore whether these are new issues or ongoing questions,
    whether folks have said these out loud before, and how they rate
    them (e.g. life changing, significant but not life-changing, annoying,
    persistent, startling or unexpected, frightening, etc.)

4) Share any pastoral materials from your church or denomination and the prepared Resource Sheet. Discuss what follow-up is necessary.

Closing Words

Let us call on our deepest faith:

>That which reassures us...
>
>That which comforts us...
>
>That which binds us to other people of faith...

If your community has a special prayer or covenant it uses regularly, invite the group to recite it here.

Let us nurture our capacity to be more

>than our needs and worries of the world.

Let us uphold each other in our search for meaning

>especially when events beyond our control confuse us.

Let us encourage each other in deepening empathy and compassion

>for victims, survivors, and each other's emotional wellbeing.

Let us bless each other in wonder of this life we share

>even when we are unsure of our own footing
>
>or anxious about loved ones and friends.

Let us challenge each other to be our best selves.

And as we heal, let us build effective systems of service and safety

>for all our neighbors.

REMEMBERING RIGHTLY

Opening Words

We remember fondly and gather in those that are absent.

It is both an honest and pleasant sentiment.

Remembering is an essential part of spirituality.

Our culture encourages us to happy reminiscing.

Our brains naturally prefer nostalgia.

But religious traditions encourage us to remember rightly:

To name our hurts and limitations and seek healing...

To name our gift and blessings and begin sharing...

To put our relationships in good order...

Let us open our hearts to hear each other's hurts *and* gifts *and*

To re-member our lives with right relationship.

In peace we pray: Amen.

Pastoral Reflection

When we bring to mind all that is troublesome:

The violence of war and rape and oppression...

The injustice of inequity and the darkness of depression...

The worries of our families and friends and folks beside us
at work or home...

We risk being absorbed in fear and the sense of futility.

Instead, *together* let us be trustees of grace.

In our meditation let us embrace these wounds only long enough
to bless them, share them, and release them.

Silent Meditation and Sharing (10 -15 min)

1st: Pose the following questions for silent meditation and journaling.
Invite sharing in groups of 3-4. Remember folks can "pass" on sharing.

- What wounds, hurts, and burdens are you carrying today?
- What healing are you working on? How are you doing it?
- What limitations do you frequently try to ignore or soft-pedal rather than admit and honor?
- What limitations have taught you something valuable? How?
- What relationship are you trying to heal and/or deepen?

Pastoral Reflection

When we bring to mind all that is delightful:

    Birthdays, weddings, anniversaries ...

    Art in the park, school concerts, dance recitals...

    Picnics on the porch, Frisbee with the dog...

    Long conversations with friends, an unexpected day off...

We risk being self-absorbed.

Instead, *together* let us be trustees of grace.

In our meditation let us embrace these delights only long enough

    to bless them, share them, and release them.

Silent Meditation and Sharing (10 -15 min)

1ˢᵗ: Pose the following questions for silent meditation and journaling.
Invite sharing in groups of 3-4. Remember folks can "pass" on sharing.

- What is your favorite celebration in the year? Why?
- If you could do whatever you wanted with a day, what would you do and who would do it with you?
- How do your favorite activities highlight your blessings and gifts?
- What blessings do you share most easily? What blessings are hard for you to share? Why?
- How do the people you love help/hinder your ability to grow and use your gifts?

Pastoral Reflection

When we bring to mind our relationships,

    we can't help but acknowledge they are complicated:

...We are blessed with friends; we are lonely.

...We are cursed with enemies; we are glad to go it alone.

...We are struggling with family; family is so easy.

We risk being sidelined.

The complications can keep us running in place.

Instead, *together* let us be trustees of grace.

In our meditation let us embrace these relationships only long enough

    to bless them, share them, and release them.

Silent Meditation and Sharing (10 -15 min)

1ˢᵗ: Pose the following questions for silent meditation and journaling.
Invite sharing in groups of 3-4. Remember folks can "pass" on sharing.

- Which relationships worry you right now? Which are healthy and happy right now?
- What relationships shaped you that still need healing?
- What relationships have been long-term blessings—even if they've had highs and lows?
- Generally, what do you need in your relationships? How do you approach people?

Closing Words

Pains, limitations, complications. Joys, gifts, possibilities.
It's no wonder that it is hard work to remember rightly
> When we can experience such a range of highs and lows!

Friends, there are so many initiatives for a better world,
> so much creativity at work for a healthier society—

We cannot afford to remember badly!
Sure, we may be burdened, but we are also gifted.
Yes, our lives are complicated, including our relationships,
> but we are also invested in reaching beyond our personal circles.

When we remember rightly who we are
> and how we are in the world, then we have much to offer:
> Gifts, skills, insight, wisdom, knowledge, realism, hope...

Share what you think you have to offer to the world...

Let us give our hearts and hands to the healing arts and to justice
> that our troubles may be transformed.

Let us remember rightly what responsibilities our blessings afford.
Let us remember rightly our liability for our lives and each other.
Let us be trustees of grace for the common good:
> Raising up the wounded, cheering the upright and hopeful,
> exposing our hidden lives to contemplation and discernment.

Rev. Dr. Claudia A. Ramisch

4 BENEDICTIONS & PRAYERS

TEACHER'S BEATITUDE BLESSING

Blest are you who are vulnerable to questions:
>Knowledge and wisdom shall be yours.

Blest are you who are grieved by disinterest:
>You shall become creative.

Blest are you with limited resources:
>You shall master innovation.

Blest are you who long for wholeness and integration:
>You model discipline, health, and balance.

Blest are you who refuse to elevate test scores and labels:
>Your students shall be liberated to learn.

Blest are you who love your students:
>You open the path of insight, growth, and skill.

Blest are you who suffer for the art and science of education:
>You foster civilization.

Blest are you when they mock you and insult you
>for your dedication and idealism.

Rejoice and be glad for you are a witness to truth, beauty, and justice.
>You have planted a tree of life in humanity's garden.

SCHOOL BLESSING FOR CHILDREN

We give thanks for the gift of these children entrusted to us.

We bless you as you begin a new school year.

May you grow in self-confidence and the skills of friendship.

May you be challenged to learn more of our world and care for it.

May you be good listeners and show respect
to teachers, staff, and classmates.

May you be cherished and protected by all charged with your care.

May you always know that you are loved and valued by us.

May you love and value this time dedicated to education. Amen.

FOR THE SUCCESS OF YOUR PROJECT

Go forth and do no harm.

Go forth and do good!

Go forth with neighbors to help you.

Go forth to help other neighbors!

Go forth that others might share our bounty.

Go forth and help them have enough and be enough.

Go forth in strength and well-being.

Go forth to teach a life of holiness and health.

Go forth that no child may be in danger or want.

*Go forth that the children and grandchildren
and great-grandchildren
May be safe and happy in the world we have inherited.*

Go forth wearing a coat of grace.

Go forth wrapped in blessing!

FOR NEWLYWEDS

God of Hope and Assurance,

You have opened ___ and ___'s hearts to a new life and new promises:

May their life together be long and fulfilling.

You have given ___ and ___ to each other in love:

May every action they do be filled with love

and remind them of You.

___ and ___ share a common commitment

to this community and Your people:

May their life together be marked by holy service.

May ___ and ___ go forth in love and peace, grace and gratitude

Assured of Your blessing and our support.

In peace we pray: *Amen.*

CANDLE LIGHTING I

We light this chalice because we are together...

Because we want to see the light in our world...

Because we want to enlarge the light within us...

Because we want to be light to the world...

Because we want to burn for justice and truth...

Because we burn in service to our neighbors and world.

CANDLE LIGHTING II

We give thanks for the needs of our community

that remind us of our common humanity.

We give thanks for the needs of humanity

that help us grow into the compassion of the Buddha,

the love of Jesus, and the charity of Mohammed.

We give thanks for the needs of our hearts

that foster our commitment to share our lives and goods.

We give thanks for the gifts of today—

Our delights, our companionship, our celebrations!

FOR EVERYONE ON MOTHER'S DAY

May our lives be signed by the sacred in all seasons
As Maid, Mother, and Crone show us grace at all ages.
May our lives be full of Kali's eternal energy and Mary's fidelity.
May our visions be as broad as Buddhamitra's and as clear as Deborah's.
May our spirits be as brave as Hypatia's,
As pure as White Buffalo Woman's,
And as free as Zora Neale Hurston's.
May our hearts always be open to the women with whom we partner
May our works always make the world safer and healthier for all –
Judging wellbeing by how women and children thrive in our midst.
May it be so!

FOR THE SPIRIT OF LISTENING

When we hear the joys and hopes,
worries and concerns of each other's hearts.
May we breathe a spirit of hope on all we have heard.
As recognition of our common humanity rises in our breasts,
May we allow the pains and desires we keep hidden
to also rise in the quiet.
In the days to come, may we hold these things
up to the light of discernment.
May we bless the gifts, sort out the useless,
and open ourselves to the Inner Voice of Conscience.

FOR THE MAN NEXT TO ME

The man next to me

Is a universe of experience needing affirmation.

The man next to me

Is outward energy, directed action, and inward question.

The man next to me

Roils with urgency and possibility.

The man next to me

Has a story to tell and an anthem to sing.

The man next to me

Desires to know and be known:

physically, mentally, emotionally, spiritually.

The man next to me

Is barely keeping things together

but continues to look out for his loved ones.

The man next to me

Lives by faith, struggles in hope, labors for love.

The man next to me

Is expected to be self-sufficient but he'd rather be a partner.

The man next to me

Is more than any description or explanation

for he is miracle and mystery.

The man next to me

Is creative, responsible, and strong.

The man next to me

Is fearfully wonderfully made and precious.

He is to be received as anointed messiah and divine masculinity.

He is to be treasured.

He is gift.

Blessed are you, my brother!

FOR THE FRUITS OF TONGLEN

As we conclude our meditation on the disquiet around us,
We dedicate its positive and healing power
to those we have visualized.
We pray that the merit of our practice of compassion
may benefit all other beings.
We extend this compassion to all who are suffering-
friends, our community, strangers, the world.
Daily, we will practice taking in
and transforming suffering into compassion.
We will extend all of our happiness, clarity, understanding,
forgiveness and love.
May all beings be happy.

FOR OUTREACH

Do not let a gulf stand between us and others of faith.
Make of yourself a bridge.
Do not confuse the destination with the journey.
Fix your eyes on the vision and your feet on the path.
Do not be hasty or hurried or haughty.
Be deliberate and humble even in uncertainty and ambiguity.
Do not fear failure or rejection.
Step out boldly clothed in your dignity and wrapped in our blessing.
Make of yourself a bridge.

CHRISTMAS EVE CANDLE LIGHTING

It is Christmas Eve; the stores have closed and the frenzy has paused.
This is not just any night.
We have gathered in a time outside of time to rest, sing, and celebrate.
This is not just any place.
Here you have sanctuary, a place apart in safety.
This is not just any crowd.
These are your community—family and friends, neighbors and visitors.
We choose to share life together in this shelter,
In this moment.
Welcome! Welcome! Welcome!
Let us consecrate this time together by lighting this chalice.
Let us savor the opportunity this time and place offer to us.
Let us be open to insight from the great winter stories,
To delight in the great festivals and traditions,
And to comfort from this sacred gathering.

FOR LABOR DAY

We have a vision of people at work using their gifts and abilities well.
We have a vision of people paid living wages.
We have a vision of people working enough to care for their families,
And not needing multiple jobs to do that.
We bless human labor: the dignity it affords, the creativity it frees,
And the meaning it offers.
We bless efforts to provide meaningful work for all citizens who are able.
We bless people struggling with unemployment and underemployment.
We bless educators and parents teaching the young a healthy work ethic
And skills for their jobs.
We bless efforts to value and respect all professions.
We bless efforts for just wages and benefits.
And we bless all enjoying the holiday and those traveling the highways.

FOR A SACRED JOURNEY

Bless your feet with oils
    that your steps may be fragrant on the earth.
Bless your mind with openness
    that your journey may be insightful.
Bless your hands with powders
    that you may surely ring the bells of delight and devotion
    at the shrines on your way.
May the sound and aroma of your passing be a blessing to kith and kin.

FOR MANY WINTER FEASTS

May you delight in our feasts
and the feasts of our neighbors and friends—and gain from each:
    May you have Bodhi spirits of persistence,
        moderation, and enlightenment.
    May you have Hanukkah hands open to miracles
        in the work of rebuilding the city.
    May you have Solstice eyes to see new light as it breaks the winter.
    May you have Yalda and Yule senses of goodness ever reborn.
    May you have Christmas ears to hear songs of hope
        and voices of righteousness.
    May you have Kwanzaa hearts that embrace values
        of health, industry, and family.
    May you have all you need to embody your deepest convictions
        even in dark and cold times.
May we join together in bringing forth the Day to Come:
    A day of peace, security, justice and generosity.

FOR A COVENANT COMMUNITY I

Let us seek out meaning together.

We will broaden our awareness and deepen our thought.

Let us wonder together.

We will be reverent before the truth of each one's thought.

All around us there is growth.

We will nurture sprouts, tend flowers, and prune dead wood.

All around us there is need.

We will be generous in charity, true in justice,

And observant of right relations with all of nature.

For right here, right now

With you in this work--

I stand in covenant.

We stand in covenant.

Even as I speak I know my mind.

Even as we sing we know our spirit.

But as I stand with you, I know God.

Blessed be, now and evermore.

FOR A COVENANT COMMUNITY II

We are people of faith covenanted in community.

May we trust each other with our dreams and work together for justice.

We are people of hope who envision a healthy and whole society.

May we remember we do not walk alone

and be courageous in pressing forward.

We are people who love our homeland and her aspirations.

May we be consistent and persistent in our attention

to the needs of our land and our people.

We are people of constancy, young in spirit and savvy in skill,

promised to future generations.

May those beyond our lives benefit from how we live today.

In peace we pray: Amen.

FOR QUESTIONS & QUESTS

We are only a moment.

    The koi and tortoise, the oak and sequoia outlive us.

    The Sphinx and Great Wall outlast us.

    The Seven Sisters outshine us.

In our hands: Naught but the illusion of control.

In our hands: Everything in part and in total.

In our hands: Questions of meaning.

In our hands: Our quest together.

May the ancestral hands we grasp,

    slip us notes with their most enduring questions on them.

May we translate those questions

    and transcribe them to pass on to the next in line.

May the life-death-power-nothing-dance and the mystery in our hands

    enhance rather than overshadow or overwhelm our dignity.

May we be grateful for our quest together for meaning

    and not just for our private questions .

May the outstretched, upturned hand we each bring with us,

    support the life we share together in peace.

May we use our gathering to shape fruitful reflection on our questions

    and all that we hold most dear.

WINTER BOWL OF LIGHT

Around this bowl of light,

    We hold each other's needs with gentleness.

Around this bowl of light,

    We delight in each other's joys.

Around this bowl of light

    We name our hopes and claim our dreams.

May this bowl of light fill our hearts

    With anticipation and commitment to new beginnings.

May this bowl of light fill our hearts

    With the comfort of community and assurance of support.

LITANY: TO BE COMPASSIONATE

Here and now: The world is in shambles.

War is too near.

Families are broken.

Children are hungry.

We are truly all of this.

Hold us surely, hold us closely.

That we may be compassionate.

Here and now: Some friends are dying.

Some are desperate.

Some are sickly.

Some are lonely and empty.

We are truly all of this.

Hold us surely, hold us closely.

That we may be compassionate.

Here and now: I was in a tailspin

But you were in the work.

I despaired of finding friendship

But you tracked me down.

We are truly all of this.

Hold us surely, hold us closely.

That we may be compassionate.

Here and now: Listen to and speak from your hearts.

Let us listen to each other's hearts.

Call a new name; meet a new person.

Be gentle with bruised hearts and kind with fragile spirits

To hold the world surely, to hold the people closely.

That we may be compassionate.

FOR CHILDREN OR FRUITFUL DISCERNMENT

May your choices be thoughtful and helpful:

May you make a difference this week.

May you have the strength to follow-through in all your work:

May your results be happy and rewarding.

EQUINOX PRAYER

The day when light and dark are perfectly matched is humanly strange.
Though we desire and pursue equilibrium,
     our lives are not usually so beautifully balanced.
Let us set free some of the light and dark we haul around within us
     that throw us off balance.
Then let us rest in the harmony nature offers us today.
It's good for us; it's good for our community.
     It's good for all we care about that we rest in harmony...
As we resume our activities in this crazy world of highs and lows,
     good and bad
May this harmony inform our choices to be invested in the wellbeing
     of even those we can't physically touch or hear.
May this gathering strengthen our investment,
     nurture our sensibilities and sensitivity to need,
     and deepen our care for the good and bad all around us.
May this time of reflection and prayer
help us extend that care beyond our own needs
     To find a way to touch those out of reach,
     To find a way to hear small voices,
     To find a way to cultivate harmony and balance for all the earth.

FOR A WEDDING

Let us pray. O Spirit of Life:
You have drawn us together today as witnesses to love.
Bless this service and the union it celebrates.
As ___ and ___ vow their lives to each other,
     May they be open and sincere of heart,
     May they have strength and clarity of mind,
     May they be generous of spirit,
     May they be prepared to be faithful in all ways to each other
          and to the vows they make today before this assembly.
As ___ and ___ enter this sacred covenant,
     may we unite in prayer and goodwill for their happiness and health.
O Spirit of Life, hear our humble prayer!

LITANY FOR PEACE

War continues. And war threatens again. And again.
And neighborhood violence mimics its pattern.

    We have a vision of a peaceful and harmonious world.

    We bless refugees and victims seeking healing and safety.

    We bless children confused and struggling
        to make sense of our fierce world.

    We bless peacekeeping forces, diplomats,
        and service personnel pursuing a nobler world.

    We bless visionaries creating peaceful societies,
        people pursuing civil discourse,
        and pacifists working to change the nature of conflict.

    We bless neighbors who refuse to engage in toxic relationships
        and who work for the safety of those in abusive situations.

Let us keep before us the vision of a world of wholeness and security,
        where all people are sheltered in holy comfort
        as they share their hearts and lives.

Let us give our lives to this vision of peace and harmony.

BLESSING WITH WATER

Water is precious.
May you know you are precious in body, mind, and spirit.
Water is part of you; in fact, it is most of you and the earth.
May you know you are deeply connected to the earth and to all creatures.
Water helps us in many ways every day: to clean, to purify, to soothe,
    to change and shape, to power, and to sustain.
May you be helped with all you need.
Water is regarded with awe and gratitude in all the world's religions.
May you know many springs of grace and knowledge are available to you.
May you drink deeply from the waters of life and love and inspiration.

Rev. Dr. Claudia A. Ramisch

5 READINGS & POEMS

POEM: YOU ARE HOPE

Like sweat from the struggle,

Hope oozed out of my pores and meaning crumbled in my marrow.

The labor was beyond me. My frame is fragile now.

I cannot go with you.

    I cannot go with you through that valley,

    Through that fog and mist, through that swirling wind.

    I cannot image a reason to study directional charts

    For I have neither the strength to shoulder a pack

        nor will to rise from this pallet.

If I thought light was returning...

If—

Perhaps I would crawl to the tent flap for a look...

Perhaps—

When you return from your journey,

Tell me about what you've found and I will be renewed.

    Tell me of your discoveries with depth and detail,

    Of paths that failed or foundered,

        of secret passwords and passages.

Tell me of stars that refused to set,

Stars that fed your perseverance as you sat at the nightly campfire

Recounting your day's events and crafting your story

    for your great-great-grandchildren.

Be faithful. Be strong.

You are hope.

READING: ALIEN

I was an alien. I knew it when I stepped out my door.

These people all around me were different and they had the advantage.

They were rich and I was poor; I felt trapped by rules.

They didn't even see me. I was a number.

They were ordinary and I was beautiful; I felt trapped by trends.

They didn't even see me. I was an image.

They were cold and I was caring; I felt trapped by neediness.

They didn't even see me. I was a role.

It didn't matter the face I showed, the goods I wore, the gifts I had;

I was trapped by my own identity.

And yes, they, they were all different than I was.

The worst of it was that they all seemed to know what they were about.

I surmised it was my alien nature that made me wonder:

What should I say? What must I do? How am I to fit in?

Have you heard or had thoughts like these?

They're not unusual perspectives; it's possible we fit in by not fitting in.

When we are teenagers, we are sure we are alien—

even if we have a crowd with which to run.

Isolation—not solitude—is both a tendency and a temptation

when we feel alien to our world…

We fear it; we use it to induce fear.

We choose it when we are in fear rather than expose our need.

When we are sick or oppressed, we are sure we are alone—

even if we have six people beside us.

Healthy differentiation gets us past our teen phase.

You know, the kind where you know yourself,

but no longer imagine the universe is yours?!

Then self-awareness grows us beyond our isolationist tendencies.

You know, that self-awareness that can honestly name needs--

without being whiny or overbearing or shutting down.

Uh oh. It just may be that the individual who is

Well differentiated and self-aware—

And able to express one's self clearly

Really is the alien.

READING: CHRISTMAS QUILT PRAYER

The night is crisp and dark. We are blessed to gather in warmth and light.
The fabric of our lives is as varied as what we use to clothe our bodies—
    some ugly, some beautiful patterns;
    some light, some stout weights; whole bolts and scraps.
We are blessed to have a veritable warehouse of fabrics
    in our gathering.
We generally use these fabrics to present ourselves to each other,
    but tonight what about making a Christmas quilt from them?
May we have the courage to share the fabrics
    of experience and meaning in which we wrap ourselves
That we may sew a pattern to ease the suffering and sickness about us…
That we may stitch together a quilt of comfort
    in sorrow and weariness…
That we may piece a quilt of sacred memory and holy aspiration
    as a gift to our children and their children's children.
In peace we pray: Amen.

READING: CHRISTMAS ANNOUNCEMENT

As people have done for centuries upon centuries:
We announce with joy: The light is returning…
    We pray that our fears be as flash paper and our worries
    be as kindling for the fire of hope.
We announce with conviction: The small and weak shan't be neglected
in a righteous world…
    We pray with all people of goodwill that we will make this so.
We announce with awe: Miracles simply use ordinary elements
in extraordinary ways…
    We pray with all crafters that our creativity ignites holy change
    with whatever is at hand.
We announce with passion: Oppression can be pushed back by justice…
    We pray with activists around the world for the strength
    to persevere in adversity.

POEM: WHO ARE YOU?

Who are You?
To meet us where we are, to know our every need—
To speak our every language, to hear our every plea—
To feel our every ache, to sing our every song—
Who are you? To hold in balance all that would singly consume us.
Who are you? To be unchanging, but not unmoved.
Who are you?
You remain undefined and undefinable.
You live unencumbered by definition or identity even as You are known.
The names by which we call You are an insult to Your self,
    But they honor our hopes and needs and experiences.
And somehow, you graciously answer
    when we hurl these insults into Your universe.
And someway You know our names though we can't pronounce Yours.
You are the One-Who-Is—
    everything else we say is speculation for our comfort.
Why do we desire and seek that comfort?
Why do we speculate, literally gamble?
Perhaps because we are only known by what we can name
    and the stories we can tell…
Forgive us for being ourselves! But You seem to like us…
Who are You? Who are You?

READING: GOODNESS

Within free will—
Knowledge of goodness is responsibility.
And this knowledge is an imperative without feeling.
Assent is a mere formality.
Denial is simply sin.
Goodness is goodness.
It is its own value.
It must be done.
There is no because.

POEM: STILLNESS

No less than six Southern Emerald moths
and no more than two square-winged dragonflies
accompanied me all the way up the lane
changing guard as they approached regularly placed
but invisible checkpoints.
The sun was waning;
the whole lane was golden as it slid to the horizon.
There were a few clouds and I anticipated brilliance
would break out at any moment.
Katydids and cicadas were holding their nightly karaoke competition.
Despite this, I can only say it was a still evening.
I looked forward to watching the sunset and returning to my silent cabin.
Suddenly, without warning,
I was body slammed by a butterfly—
I suspected a Dull Firetip.
I was a giant in comparison.
I couldn't help but laugh out loud destroying the reverie
but not the reverence.

READING: COMMUNITY IS SOUL SPACE

Humans are relational and we are constantly buffeted by our relationships. The dynamic of the world keeps us bouncing around. If we want our shy souls to have even a fighting chance, we have to *create* welcoming conditions for them. When we give our shy souls this attention and space, they transform us *and* our relationships.

Soul spaces are often identified with beautiful natural settings. These are good for us and we should enjoy them as fully as possible. But we should not confuse them with formation for soul living. If we want to live an undivided life, we must allow our souls to have their space in community because soul *living* isn't all about me—it's engaged with you, them, us... Formation in soul living is deliberate and hard community work.

READING: RISE IN HOPE

When we name our pains, when we claim our losses,
    when we admit our griefs, we open the door to hope.
And when we refuse to let the pains, losses, and griefs be the whole story,
    Hope walks in.
Hope is the awareness that there is more—more justice than we live,
    more love than we can express, more life than we can see or imagine.
Hope is also the force that capitalizes on this awareness.
It acknowledges that life is not fair and doesn't buckle.
It prompts innovative and persistent action for change for everyone.
As hope grapples with the present
    it does not postpone life into the future.
And hope is not a private stash of spiritual resources
    but a community supply.
Hope is a theological commons—
    like water, land, and air are ecological commons.
If we have that unalloyed view of reality
    it isn't just because we're human— It's because we have learned
    to integrate our perspective with other's views and insights.
Effectively, hope is tested and tried and hammered into a useful tool
    not in adversity and the extreme age, but in relationship.
When we say death is definitive but not final,
    pain is natural but suffering is a choice...
    We rise in hope.
When we live in and through the struggle *now*
    and refuse to be sucked into futurisms...
When we remember that this trouble is new to us,
    but the community holds a memory of how to live through it...
    We rise in hope.
When we note that Jesus, Buddha, Mahavir, and Schweitzer
    are in a line of worthy teachers pushing us
    to live beyond even evil, torture, and death into the promise of life:
    We rise in hope.
Rise in hope!

May your hope be large and persistent
    without delusions about the obstacles you face.
May you be sturdy and lasting in your practice
    for others will need you as much as you need them.
Indeed may you practice hope by engaging reality
    and shaping a world that works for all.

POEM: SWEET INNOCENCE

God of sweetness, God of sorrow,
By weaving hope into power
Dark yields dreamings of tomorrow
Clear as bell chimes from a tower.
    God of glory, God of pain,
    Filling what had once seemed hollow,
    Silent tears like winter rain
    Mark an unmarked trail to follow.
God of wisdom, God of risk,
Turning stones and baking bread—
Earth is tilled by spinning disk;
Trust the hidden till we're fed.
    God of sweetness, God of sorrow,
    You are all that I desire.
    Who are you that I should borrow
    Simple flesh to carry fire?

POEM: SPRING HAIKUS

An old winter storm
Disguised as a Spring torrent
Wraps the day in gray.

    Nature hurts nature
    As it rains and blows sideways
    While cold struts about.

Buds looked so hopeful
But ice darts through the raindrops
Arresting all growth.

    Grace is not confused
    By weath'ring contradictions
    But intellect is.

Is it possible
That great transformations are
Hidden in this gray?

    Winter to springtime
    Is dormancy converted
    To abundancy.

The gray is unwrapped
And the seeds of new season
Are surely tucked in.

    Grace is not confused
    By weath'ring contradictions
    But intellect is.

READING: INTERFAITH HERMENEUTICAL ISSUES

Healthy suspicion is like healthy skepticism: It points to important new insights about traditions—but we sometimes let it go too far and fall into cynicism and noxious spirituality. Healthy empathy is like good journalism— it asks strong questions but respects the speaker's limitations. But when we let it go too far, we accept half-answers and half-truths and remain an inch deep.

In woundedness we often confuse the message of a tradition with some of its practitioners—we become suspicious of the wrong thing; we become critical of an institution and take it out on folks who find it valuable and viable; we refuse to listen with openness to scriptures or teachers rather than deepen our study or examine the breadth of every tradition that expands beyond law and institution to mysticism and justice. We should be reminded of the general premise of interfaith work: Do not compare your best with their worst.

By accepting all inspired scriptures—including those without canon and with non-linguistic expressions— we give ourselves a monumental task in hermeneutics. We must actually know something about what we're saying about the traditions and stories we reference and be clear about how we use them so as not to do violence to their meanings or interpretations. Conversely, we must be careful how we comment on another's use of stories when they actually are working within a tradition. (e.g. I have a right to my *opinions* about what's happening in physics, but realistically they are of limited value because I am not a physicist!) When we study scriptures, we tend to be interested in knowing *about* rather than *living within* them...

Whatever scripture we accept personally—Koran or Kerouac—we need to be both invested in it and serious about its application. If we aren't we simply become the stereotype of nice, hippie types that talk a lot but don't really do much except set themselves apart as superior.

ABOUT THE AUTHOR

CLAUDIA A. RAMISCH is a hermit-wannabe originally from Maumee, OH and has been in Owensboro, KY, since 1991. She has been at the Unitarian Universalist Congregation of Owensboro since 1999 beginning as a guest speaker once a month and adding duties until being called and ordained by the Congregation in 2008.

She holds a Doctor of Ministry from Eden Theological Seminary, St. Louis (Adult Formation), a Master of Arts in Theology from Loyola of Chicago (Systematics), a Bachelor of Arts in Religious Studies (Scripture) and a Bachelor of Individualized Studies (Psychology) from Lourdes College, Sylvania OH.

Claudia has been in ministry since 1981 working with all ages from pre-school to adult, doing everything from shoveling the roof (in Sault Ste. Marie) to teaching college (Brescia University) all in the name of community life and growth. Her service has been throughout the middle states (Ohio, Indiana, Illinois, Michigan, Kentucky, and Tennessee).

Along the line, Claudia has also managed a dental practice, worked in a grocery store accounting office, and worked in an independent bookstore to continue the habit of eating.

Currently, Claudia lives in a converted garage with a Boxarotdor (Boxer-Rotweiller/Labrador mix) named Solomon; someday it will be a hermitage.

Made in the USA
Lexington, KY
02 December 2013